CONTENTS

Locales of thirty-two full-page pictures

HOLLAND: INDUSTRIOUS LAND BELOW THE SEA

"I STRUGGLE and emerge" is the proud motto of one of Holland's provinces, symbolized by a rampant lion coming forth from the ocean waves with a mighty tread. That is the story of Holland's centuries-long war against the sea, a battle that surges with the rhythm of the tides, leaving its mark not only on the contours of the reclaimed land but on the irrepressible Dutch spirit. "God made the world with the exception of Holland, which was made by the Dutch," they'll tell you.

This extraordinary man-made country is officially known as the Netherlands, for the name "Holland" originally designated only one province of the land. On the map of Europe it is a triangular pocket-country alternately caressed and assaulted by the North Sea, bordered by Belgium and Germany, in the northeast corner of the continent. About the size of Maryland, the Netherlands is only 120 miles wide and 200 miles long, with a fifth of its acreage still under water. To its eleven provinces, a twelfth—Flevoland (FLEH-*voh-lahnd*)—is now being added through amazing feats of land reclamation.

MANY-SIDED CONTRASTS

Chances are you know Holland chiefly by its familiar emblems: windmills, wooden shoes, baggy pantaloons and lace bonnets, tulip bulbs, the Flying Dutchman and the boy with his finger in the dike. It is also the multifaceted country of pastries, fish and cheese, superb diamond cutters, dynamic enterprise and stoic calm, a mosaic of floral color reflecting the artistry of Rembrandt and Vermeer.

Blending the centuries, ancient moated castles may be observed along with huge industrial centers, young farm settlements, the coal mines of the south and the meadows rich with cattle in the north. Besides being the flower, fruit and vegetable garden of Europe, Holland happens to be a leading supplier of dairy products, a great shipbuilding nation and a growing industrial power, producing everything from nuclear reactors to vitamins and varnishes.

GLORY OF THE PAST

When you walk the streets of Holland today, you may get a thrill in the thought that you're treading in the footsteps of the Gauls, the Celts, the Saxons and the Franks. When Julius Caesar's Roman legions invaded these lowlands, they found scattered farms already 400 years old, peopled by tribes of Gallic and Germanic stock. For centuries these hardy folk had been battling the sea for the possession of the land and their right to live there by fishing and raising simple crops.

In its earliest days, the Netherlands was a vast swamp, the battleground of angry seas and flooded rivers. Dike building having started as far back as the year 1000, villages sprang up with names ending in *dam:* Rotterdam, Amsterdam, Edam. Dike-building armies and windmills for pumping water spread throughout the area.

After suffering at least fifteen military invasions in as many centuries, the real history of the Netherlands began to take shape. Then, in the sixteenth century, the menace of Spain gave birth to the true spirit of freedom which made the Dutch a great nation and paved the way for Holland's Golden Age. At that time, Holland was a group of autonomous countries, duchies and cities known as the Nether (low) Lands. They rose up against Spanish domination in a bitter eighty-year war for freedom of religious belief, and in a revolution behind the driving force of William the Silent became the Republic of the United Netherlands.

In the Golden Century of the 1600's, the country flourished. This tiny nation had a vitality that nothing could conquer—not the encroaching seas, nor the mighty Spanish Empire, nor the bitter religious strife of the Reformation. Practical but daring, the Dutch turned to exploration and foreign trade, and their sailing vessels ranged the seven seas. These were years of discovery—the fabulously rich East Indies, Africa, the New World—and the orange flag of the Dutch fleet fluttered over the Hudson River, over Tasmania and New Zealand and New Guinea. The Bank of Amsterdam was the richest in the world, and Holland was queen of the seas.

There was wealth, too, of another kind—for this was the age of ideas and art, of Spinoza and Rembrandt. Here was a haven for exiles and religious dissenters, among them the English Pilgrims who were soon to sail across the Atlantic in the *Mayflower* to a less friendly shore.

Eventually England gained supremacy of the seas and of some Dutch colonies as well. But Holland remained wealthy and independent until the years of the Napoleonic invasion, when it became a pawn of greater powers. Within twenty years, however, the Dutch regained their sovereignty and established the Kingdom of the Netherlands, with a written constitution assuring the rights of its citizens.

St. Nicholas visits every town in Holland, rewarding the good children with gifts on December 6.

During the First World War Holland remained neutral, but in the holocaust of World War II it was trampled by invading Nazi armies and many of its greatest cities were almost obliterated by bombing raids. Characteristic of the Dutch, when the first Jews were seized the whole city of Amsterdam went on strike, and it was there that the young Anne Frank wrote her inspiring diary. The people's love of freedom, spurred by the German occupation, produced an army of fanatical resistance fighters to plague the conquerors until the Liberation. When peace came, Holland resolutely set to work rebuilding its cities and its ancient dikes, destroyed by bombs and retreating armies.

Today Holland is a prosperous member of the European community, and belongs to the North Atlantic Treaty Organization and the United Nations.

THE DUTCH TOUCH

Clearly the role played by the Dutch in history has been out of all proportion to the size of the midget country. By now, although Holland has lost most of its colonies, the Dutch influence is visible in architecture, home furnishings and in gardens everywhere. But above all else, it is in the world of art that Dutch genius has been felt. Masters like Rembrandt and Frans Hals, whose works are avidly collected today, painstakingly represented texture, surface and diffusion of light in their magnificent canvases.

In the governmental archives at the Hague is a letter, dated November 5, 1626, from a delegate of the Dutch West Indies Company: "Our people have purchased the island of Manhattan from the Indians for the value of 60 guilders." This easy acquisition of the island on which the skyscrapers of New York now reach toward the sky cannot be compared to the cost of acquiring the coastal lands, the dunes, the small farm areas that make up the Netherlands. Many acres of these lands were gained through the tremendous effort of walling out the sea, reclaiming fertile ground from the bottom of a lake, dredging, dumping, filling and building protective dikes wide enough to serve as highways.

As long ago as the year 1 A.D. early people in this area were building walls as protection against the sea. Although methods have changed and machinery has been developed to help with the work, the fight to save the land from the sea and from flooding rivers has gone on continuously for centuries.

Love of this hard-won land is expressed in the clean cities, the small prosperous farms, the architecture and the art of a creative people.

A WARM AND FRIENDLY PEOPLE

At first they may strike you as shy and stolid, these Dutch, probably because of their long suffering in the struggle for survival against the sea. Yet they know how to be happy and to make others happy in simple ways—with song, laughter and good food. As an example of their good-humored attitude toward visitors, at Oudewater (ow-*deh-vah-tehr*), which lies between The Hague and Utrecht, you can be weighed on medieval scales and be given a duly attested certificate solemnly declaring that you are not a witch or a wizard.

Today, there are some 11,500,000 people in the tight little country, one of the most densely populated areas on earth—901 to every square mile, compared to 52 in the United States. Nevertheless, the Dutch have the world's longest life expectancy, the lowest death rate and the highest birth rate, largely because of their highly developed health and social security systems.

As a people, the Dutch are exceedingly practical, earthy in their honesty, hard-working and uncommonly law-abiding. Although innately conservative in clinging to old habits, they are far from reactionary. These qualities all add up to their strongly marked character, unlike that of any other people in Europe.

For over seventy years, the monarch of the Netherlands has been a woman, first Queen Wilhelmina, and after her abdication her daughter Juliana. This accident of succession has undoubtedly reinforced the traditional Dutch regard for home and family. Certainly the Dutch housewife reigns like a queen in her household. She takes great pride in keeping her home immaculate and smoothly run, needing few outside distractions.

In their homes the Dutch seldom curtain their large, flower-

To these children, a Dutch treat is a piece of pastry, rolled and raisined or twisted and sugary.

bedecked windows. They have nothing to hide and want to be hospitable to all comers. If you're lucky enough to be entertained in a Dutch home, you'll be struck by an unhurried interest in your welfare. Soon you'll be offered a cup of tea or coffee with a cookie, a bit of their rich, out-of-this-world pastry, and some of their world-famous chocolates. Then you'll be offered another cup and perhaps a raisin bun. As your visit continues you will become aware that, hardworking as the Dutch are, the spirit of unhurried calm prevails within the home.

You'll leave that Dutch house warmed by the air of family snugness, a homely conviviality that the Hollanders call *gezelligheid (kuh-*ZELL*-luk-hate)*. The word means everything that makes staying at home a pleasure. The Dutch, for instance, seldom speak loudly, nor is their music ever noisy. Adding to the coziness is the presence of the whole immediate family—*gezin (kuh-*ZEEN*)*. This word means just the husband, wife and children, not other relatives.

THE SPIRIT OF HOLLAND

One quality that stands out among the Dutch is a pervading sense of serenity and peace. You find it when sight-seeing in the picturesque villages of Volendam (*foh-len-*DAHM) or Spakenburg (SPAH-*ken-burk*), with their colorful costumes and strange customs; in the vast tulip fields of Haarlem (HAHR-*lem*); in windmills silhouetted against a sun-

set sky; in the fishing towns of Hoorn (HOHRN) and Enkhuizen (*enk-*
HOY-*zen*), and even in metropolitan shops and business offices.

Here are people who refuse to hurry or to be harried. Although
they're efficient, they never think "time is money." Somehow their
sixty-minute hour has space in it for daily living. On most people, the
serene contentment of Holland has a tranquilizing effect.

Yet the Dutch, stubbornly surviving a dramatic succession of invasions, rebellions and liberations, have produced a country exciting in
its constant surprises to travelers. One day you may gaze at a thirteenth-century church, the Oude Kerk (ow-*deh kehrk*) in Delft, and
the next day you may step straight out of the Middle Ages to stare at
the *avant-garde* edifices of resurrected Rotterdam. Nearby, a staid,
well-dressed businessman may pause with utter dignity to swallow a
salted herring at a street stall.

Holland, the new and the old, the gay and the somber, is that full
of wonders. So let's take a trip, starting appropriately with the most
important of all Dutch cities, the glorious and improbable capital of
the Netherlands, the floating city called Amsterdam.

Tree-lined canals and gabled roofs form the pattern of old Amsterdam, the "Venice of the North."

let's travel in

HOLLAND

AMSTERDAM: CHURCHES AND THE SEA

IN THIS imposing view of Amsterdam, we see the oldest part of the historic port city, where the Ijssel (EYE-*ssel*) River empties into the old Zuider Zee (ZIGH-*der* ZAY). Towering above the ancient dockside is the relatively modern Church of St. Nicholas, built in 1886. It is one of several churches in the capital dedicated to the city's patron saint, who has long been popular with both Protestant and Catholic sailors all along the seacoast.

Directly below the tallest tower you can see a low, circular building known as the "Weeping Tower," which dates back to 1482. Here, in the days when Holland's fleet was conquering far-off lands, the wives and children of daring seafarers came to bid farewell for long years and often forever.

Ships and churches have molded Amsterdam, and all of Holland. The blending of the Dutch way of life with their religion has left an architectural heritage. In almost every city and town you'll find the strength and harmony of a semicircular Romanesque chapel, the graceful peaked arches and spires of a Gothic edifice or the classical beauty of a Renaissance church.

Although World War II destroyed many of the beautiful Netherlands churches, hundreds remain, some of them ten centuries old. At Maastricht (*mahs*-TRICKT), for example, in the southeastern corner of the country, the Church of St. Servatius, begun in the sixth century, is the oldest in all Holland. In the center of the Netherlands, at Utrecht, is the mighty tower of the Domkerk, its cathedral spire the highest among the many which adorn Dutch cities. The forty-two bells of the open octagonal chime tower ring out above the Gothic church, which was begun in the thirteenth century.

Holland's churches are not only real architectural treasures, they are full of the country's history.

THE GRACHTEN: NETWORK OF CANALS

IF YOU want to see Amsterdam at its most delightful, there's no better way than from the water. One of the enchantments of Amsterdam is its *grachten* (KRAHK-*ten*), the wonderful network of waterways that winds through the city. Take one of the boats shown in this picture, and you'll cruise through all the important canals of Amsterdam.

Glide along near the fascinating labyrinths of narrow streets under centuries-old bridges, beneath the branches of tall elms, past stately patrician homes built by the merchant princes of the seventeenth and eighteenth centuries and now mostly used as banks or office buildings. Suddenly turning a corner, you may come across a gray old church at the end of a quiet canal, and the tinkling chimes of the carillon will sound in your ears like silver bells. Later, when you reach the broad waters of the Ijssel River, you'll see the ocean liners berthed in the docks.

At any season, these forty canals are an ever-changing source of beauty. You get the impression that Amsterdam is like a dream city floating upon a huge lake. It has over four hundred bridges—even more than Venice. Amsterdam is, in fact, cut up into ninety islands, each

High fashion in the Netherlands capital works its universal magic on women of all ages.

firmly anchored on a solid foundation of wooden piles. As any schoolboy can tell you, the Royal Palace rests securely on 13,659 piles. You'll agree that Amsterdam, as you see it from these amazing canals, is one of the wonders of the world.

18

THE
LEIDSEPLEIN:
NIGHT LIFE ON
THE AMSTEL

AFTER a rain the neon-lit heart of Amsterdam can only hint at the exciting night life in the gay capital. Hollanders have always known how to enjoy themselves. The entertainment mecca of Amsterdam is the glowing, cosmopolitan Leidseplein (*laid-seh*-PLAIN), shown here on an uncommonly quiet evening. A miniature combination of Times Square and Piccadilly Circus, it is lively by day or night, and it has something to please every taste.

Concentrated in the area—which flanks the Singelgracht (SING-*el-krahkt*), one of the outer canals—are elegant night clubs with international floor shows, smart bars, terraced restaurants with peerless dance bands, movie houses and quiet spots for mood music. Here, too, is the Municipal Theatre, where many of Holland's chief dramatic and operatic productions are staged.

The café is an integral part of an Amsterdamer's life, particularly in summer on the Leidseplein. At these cafés, you'll see many students and artists—or those who look like students and artists—along with more average citizens. People passing by peer into the cafés unselfconsciously to see who's inside and to wave at acquaintances. A young man may leave his work at about five, go home to his apartment, have dinner and then take his wife out to one of the cafés on the Leidseplein for coffee. After an hour or two, they get up, take a stroll and then go home to bed.

DUTCH FOOD: ADVENTURES FOR GOURMETS

AT ANY good restaurant in Holland, such as this one, your mouth will water at the sight of a savory spread. Amsterdam, particularly, is a city of gourmets. You can choose from an assortment of Italian, French, Swiss, Chinese, Spanish, Jewish and, of course, Dutch cuisine.

But the rare adventure is the famous rijsttafel (RAIST-*tahf'l*), or rice table. This prodigious meal, served not only in Amsterdam restaurants but all over the country, originated in the Indies and consists of some thirty-five different dishes, including from twenty to sixty condiments —some sharp, some sweet, others sour. The main dish is rice, with your choice of fried chicken, vegetables, tiny red fish, pork, miniature meat balls, salads, shrimp, fried bananas and chutneys. Pick your condiments carefully to keep your tongue from burning or the tears from streaming down your face.

Hollanders love beans with bacon, a mixture of kale and potatoes with smoked sausage, and particularly pea soup, which appears regularly on every dinner menu. This thick soup, called *snert* (SNARED), is prepared with pork, sausage and a secret selection of vegetables, and allowed to cook overnight. Among other Dutch specialties are fruit tarts, tiny cream puffs, cheese wafers, and special pastry sticks called *krakelingen* (KRAH-*kel-ling-en*).

The Dutch really enjoy their food—and so will you. Say the Dutch equivalent of delicious —*"lekker, so lekker"* (LECK-*k'r*, *soh* LECK-*k'r*)—to your waiter, and watch him smile.

East Indian waiters serve a bewildering array of dishes at the rijsttafel. Best combination: a little of everything.

22

THE
RIJKSMUSEUM:
REMBRANDT'S
"NIGHT WATCH"

FEW countries are more prolific in art galleries and museums than the Netherlands. For the lover of art, the main attraction in Amsterdam is the Netherlands National Gallery, the Rijksmuseum (RAIKS-*mew-zeh-ewm*), which proudly displays one of the best and largest collections of Dutch masterpieces in existence. Among them is this memorable Rembrandt canvas, *Night Watch*.

This painting is of such startling beauty that you may find it hard to tear yourself from it. Covering an entire wall in one gallery, *Night Watch* seems to come more alive on every visit. All day long, parties of foreigners and Dutch schoolchildren stand solemnly in front of the masterpiece, which has been called "the most valuable painting in the world." Yet this remarkable work was considered so outlandish in its day that the very men who had commissioned it as a group portrait refused to accept the canvas. Rembrandt's prestige fell, and the years that followed were marked by poverty and despair. Time has proved how wrong were the haughty men who live today in this great masterpiece.

The Rijksmuseum also contains other Dutch paintings from the fifteenth to the nineteenth century, including works by Frans Hals, Jan Vermeer and Jan Steen. But it is Rembrandt who is the chief magnet, for he was endowed with an eye that saw deeply into the faces he painted. His self-portraits are the most moving, for he searched his own countenance to reach the soul.

Besides the Dutch masters, the National Gallery displays other riches—precious furniture of all periods, tapestries, glassware, Delftware, and medieval sculpture.

DIAMOND CUTTING: THE MASTER CRAFTSMEN

THE young woman in this picture is using a magnifying glass to marvel at an exquisitely wrought gem produced by the veteran diamond cutter at the bench. Many famous stones have been cut and polished here in Amsterdam, which ranks with Antwerp as a world-famous center of the diamond industry. During the last war, the Amsterdam industry suffered great losses when the Germans carried off whole plants and deported many Jewish diamond workers. But after liberation the industry was immediately rebuilt and a special training school founded for diamond cutters.

Today, you can watch the fascinating process of diamond cutting merely by arranging for a visit to one of these establishments through the official Dutch travel bureau.

Making a rough diamond look like an exquisite jewel involves sawing, cutting for form and polishing. For the sawing, the master craftsmen use a fast-revolving, circular copper saw rimmed with diamond dust, because only a diamond can cut another diamond. In cutting for form, the artisan makes either the "emerald cut" (squarish, with graduated facets like stair-steps) or the "brilliant," which has exactly fifty-eight facets no matter how much or how little it weighs. The most valuable diamonds are those that are rose-colored; the blue-white are next in value.

If you're in luck when you're in Holland, there may be a diamond exhibition going on in Amsterdam. Roam around it among millions of dollars' worth of gems, varying in size from that of a starling's egg to virtually invisible specks of brilliance. Pause to look over the shoulder of one of the cutters at work; with a magnifying glass, you can count the fifty-eight facets. Undoubtedly, these Amsterdam diamond cutters are superlative artisans.

FRIESLAND: PROVINCE OF SKATERS

EVERYONE in Holland owns a pair of ice skates. That's because the countless rivers, canals, marshes and lakes make ice skating a national pastime. With the heavy frosts, schools and universities grant "ice vacations," merchants forsake their shops, doctors take time off between calls to skate on the ice. The custom is for young betrothed couples to go from Amsterdam or The Hague to Gouda (GOW-*dah*), where they buy a long clay pipe for the groom, and they must bring it back without breaking the pipe—ice skating all the way—to ensure a happy marriage.

Up north, in the province of Friesland (FREES-*lahnd*) where this picture was taken, the lakes are frozen longer than they are elsewhere in Holland. Here, when work on the farms comes to a standstill, people slip on a pair of skates and set out on a visiting tour of relatives and friends.

Back in 1890, a Dutch sports writer decided he'd try to cover all eleven towns in the province—a distance of 125 miles along canals and lakes connecting the towns—in one day. He did it in less than thirteen hours. Since then, the tradition of the Eleven Towns skating event has developed; whenever there's a severe frost, a race over the route is staged. Thousands of contestants and spectators gather in a festive mood and the tracks are decorated with flags showing the way. The race is so grueling that sometimes the winner lands in a hospital with frostbitten toes.

While many of the contestants use all-steel skates screwed under their shoes, the majority still stick to the old-fashioned wooden variety strapped to their shoes with strong laces, while the really conservative Frisians skate in their stockinged feet with the skates strapped on loosely, like slippers. Yet they glide along with amazing speed. Among the racers are lawyers, butcher boys, mayors, street sweepers, and even some brave women. Not all get to the finish line, but in this Dutch marathon it's the sporting spirit that counts.

THE DIKES:
RAMPARTS
AGAINST
DISASTER

HE WHO cannot master the sea," says a Dutch proverb, "is not worthy of the land." In their relentless, recurring battles against the savage, quixotic sea, rugged Hollanders have been building dikes for centuries. If it weren't for the thousand miles of dikes and dunes along the coast, almost half the nation—below sea level—would either cease to exist or be regularly flooded at every high tide.

The dike in this picture stretches twenty miles across the neck of the Zuider Zee (Southern Sea), a shallow bay of the North Sea. It has turned the Zuider Zee into a fresh-water lake known as Ijsselmeer (EYE-*ssel-mehr*). This extraordinary wall of fortress Holland rises to about twenty-four feet above sea level and also serves as a highway from the mainland.

Building dikes involves a complex process of dredging, dumping of sand and clay, laying of willow "mattresses" and final construction with stone or concrete. In recent years, Dutch techniques have been revolutionized. Nylon has proved superior to jute for sandbags and to willow mats for mattress foundations, and plastics are a good substitute for basalt rock.

The new methods are being used in Holland's latest, largest and most ambitious hydraulic project—the $600,000,000 Delta Plan, a long-range engineering job that will close up the sea arms on the southwest coast in the next twenty years. It will mean about twenty miles of new super-dikes raised in the open sea, amidst strong tidal currents, and strengthening of existing dikes so that they form an impregnable second line of defense. The Delta Plan will be a mighty rampart, the absolute defense against disasters like the 1953 flood.

Other great feats of Dutch hydraulic engineering have already aroused the world's admiration. The new Delta Plan will hold its own even beside such wonders as the Pyramids, the Eiffel Tower and the Hoover Dam in the American West.

THE POLDERS: EPIC ENTERPRISE

THE country we've taken you to is largely artificial, for the Dutch discovered long ago that useless tidelands can be turned into good soil by draining. In this heavily populated nation, with its marshes, bogs and lakes, the constant cry has been for more and more living space. To answer the demand, Hollanders have been winning new soil from water beds ever since the tenth century, adding over 2,000 square miles of habitable land which the Dutch have worked and developed with amazing zeal.

From this reclaimed soil have come watertight compartments called polders (POHL-*ders*), containing farms like the one shown on this page. Flowers and vegetables have sprung up, and the polders have been turned into the granary of the Netherlands. Lush meadows serve the famous Dutch cattle for the thriving dairy industry. Whole towns, carefully planned, have mushroomed where once there was nothing.

Today, the Dutch are gradually creating an entirely artificial twelfth province, Flevoland, with polders. By 1980, the cultivable area of the Netherlands will have increased by about a tenth, with living and working space for at least 300,000 people in the onetime bed of the disappearing Zuider Zee.

In the polder country, the water is drained into canals which serve for transportation. In many polder villages there's only one firm street, which leads to the "outer world," while internal transport is by boat.

Vast stretches of new polderland have wedded the former island of Urk to the mainland.

WONDERFUL WINDMILLS: LANDSCAPE AT KINDERDIJK

NO SCENE in Holland is lovelier than a windmill silhouetted against a sunset sky. It has become a national symbol. The graceful windmills in this picture are at Kinderdijk (*kin-der*-DAIK), southwest of Amsterdam, where nineteen of them constantly attract sight-seers.

Today there are still about thirteen hundred working windmills officially registered in the Netherlands, mostly deep in the countryside, though some are along modern highways. Some are still primitive, spreading huge wings made of fabric tautly stretched on wooden frames. The more modern are electrically operated, connected with important systems of floodgates.

While the ever-present windmills give the nation its special charm and character, they have long served the vital function of draining a country constantly threatened by the sea. The earliest windmills utilized the wind's power to grind meal, and today, many continue as "corn windmills" or "industrial mills."

Certain windmills are decorated with a traditional star motif, in gold or red, or in blue and white; the timber work of polder mills is usually green, combined with white or some other light color for the framework. For centuries, millers have been using a "sail code," by which they pass information on from mill to mill. Generally, they convey sentiments for celebrations or mourning, or a miller can pass the word that he is prepared to accept more work for his corn windmill.

The coming of an increasing number of motor-powered and electric pumping stations has not yet sounded the death knell of the windmill. For what is Holland without its windmills? Their strangely human arms beckon attention for miles around.

34

HINDELOOPEN: TIME STANDS STILL

MOVING on to strange Hindeloopen (HIN-*deh-loh-pen*), up north in the province of Friesland, we come upon this idyllic scene showing two men carrying turkeys across a bridge. This area is famous for its pedigreed black and white cattle, as well as for its turkeys. Curiously, the turkey is not very popular in Holland, even for holidays, but the Dutch raise them for export. The women in the picture are wearing their famous and exquisite costumes, with the extraordinary headgear—a cross between a bonnet and a top hat—covering their shorn hair. Among the well-to-do, the gold-headed pins at each side of the hat are diamond-studded.

People here in Friesland Province live in huge house-barns; the house is in the front and the barn in the rear. Hindeloopen, once an important port on the Zuider Zee, is now a charming relic, its main business the making of gaily painted red and blue furniture and other woodwork. Their art stems from the days when mariners stayed home all winter, passing the time in painting and carving, decorating everything from doors to tabletops and cradles. The designs, taken from the forms and colors that the sailors saw during their long journeys, mingle Norwegian and Swedish motifs with figures admired on Chinese pottery or Malayan silks.

The people in Hindeloopen, as in the rest of the province, still speak "Frisian," which is more like Anglo-Saxon than Dutch. On their clothes, identifying symbols mark the individual's place in the social structure of the community, the marital status or religious denomination. At entrancing Hindeloopen, time has little meaning.

NATIONAL COSTUMES: TRADITION AT MARKEN

COME along with us now to the former island of Marken (MARK'N), eight miles from Amsterdam, over a dike which joins it to the mainland. In this picture, you see a typical smiling Marken housewife in her weekend costume. Naturally tourists flock to the community, and the doll in the woman's arms is the sort travelers take home as a souvenir.

Marken's regional costumes are more vivid than others. In a rash of color, women wear several layers of long skirts and over-aprons, tightly laced corsets, and a variety of headgear, including the inverted bowl on this matron, with an escaping curl on each side. Men wear knee-length full breeches and tight vests, often decorated with silver buttons. Men and children walk in expensive *klompen* (KLOHM-*pen*), or wooden shoes, but usually the women go in for sensible, low-heeled black boots. It's quite a sight to watch a farmer wearing clumsy clogs, pedaling along on his bike, balancing a full pail of fresh milk.

Almost every province has its characteristic dress. In the nearby village of Volendam women go corsetless, revealing the forms nature gave them, their attire subdued in tone and less complicated. The distin-

Schoolgirls in Zeeland manage to concentrate, despite their distractingly pretty headdresses.

guishing headgear of Volendam is a three-pointed white cap. At Scheveningen (SKAY-*veh-ning-en*), women wear red, pink or blue capes. At pious Spakenburg, another costume village, the women's hair is worn in a big roll at the top of the brow and dresses look like sacks.

DELFT:
GEM
OF A CITY

WE'VE come now to the city of Delft, lying between The Hague and Rotterdam. One of the most intimate of Holland's water towns, Delft has often been described as a "small gem on Holland's landscape." That may be because its tree-lined canals are narrower than in other cities such as Amsterdam, its houses seem smaller, and its high, arched bridges are modest in size.

One of Delft's illustrious sons was the great artist Jan Vermeer. Lovers of art, lingering as they stroll through the cobblestoned streets, are apt to recognize many of the buildings and canals painted by Vermeer, for they are still unchanged. Thus a visit to Delft is a journey backward through time.

You'll sense that Delft retains the atmosphere and character of a seventeenth-century Dutch town. Its spacious market square is surrounded by picturesque old houses, and many fine mansions are mirrored in the waters of the quiet canals. It is also the historic town of William the Silent, Holland's national hero, who lived at a monastery—now the Prinsenhof (PRIN-*sen-hohf*) Museum—while in hiding, and finally was assassinated there.

As in other Dutch cities, cyclists swarm the streets. In a flat country like Holland, bicycling is the ideal means of transportation. You see cyclists everywhere: in the cities they are like a daring circus act as they maneuver through heavy traffic, dodging cars with incredible skill and oblivious of possible danger to life and limb. And since bicycling is a national sport, a web of special cycle paths spreads all over the country, providing a wonderful way to become intimately acquainted with Holland.

DELFT BLUE: CHERISHED PORCELAIN

A VISIT to Delft will inevitably bring you to one of the producers of the world-famous handmade Royal Blue Delftware. Made in this town for centuries, the cherished chinaware can be bought in many shops, and old masterpieces can be seen in breath-taking collections at two museums.

The porcelain makers of Delft long ago invented an enamel made of tin that gives their products a rare brilliance, depth and softness of color. In their graceful designs, the artists were inspired by objects brought home by Dutch sailors from far-off Japan and China. This picture shows a Dutch craftsman hand-painting a piece of fine Delft pottery. In recent years, modern designs have been added to the traditional. You'll notice that the so-called "blue" designs are actually painted on in black; they turn blue after transparent glazing and baking in an oven, when a chemical process changes the color. All these Dutch artisans retain their three secrets: the actual color, the mixing of the clay for the porcelain and the method of decoration.

Not all Delftware is blue. Among the varieties are the rich red-blue-and-gold effects of Japanese origin; the cloisonné with its crystallized glazes; the turquoise-blue which reflects the Persia of the fourteenth century; the red cracked glaze of the Ming and Ch'ing dynasties of China; and even the velvety white Delft treasured by collectors—all a remarkable demonstration of Dutch versatility.

Elsewhere in Holland, you'll find other evidence of traditional fine Dutch handicrafts, such as the exquisite glass of Leerdam (*lehr*-DAHM), the filigreed silver work of Schoonhoven (SKOHN-*hoh-ven*), the decorative brown and buff pottery at Gouda. All these, as well as the unique porcelain of Delft, are so beautiful that one realizes that there's much more to Dutch art than just the Rembrandt period.

STREET ORGAN: MUSIC IN THE AIR

NOWHERE else but in Holland can you see and hear barrel organs like this. Here the scene is Delft, though you can also find such fascinating music makers in Amsterdam and other Dutch cities. It's a peculiar Dutch institution, this magnificent, ornate organ with a great façade of carved white wood. You hear it play waltzes, Dutch clog dances and mock-Spanish tangos as well as Verdi and Puccini.

The massive musical instruments are wound with the full force of one arm and usually they are surrounded by children, some of whom dance spontaneously. Tunes gay or sad eddy through the streets, the organ giving an unmistakable Dutch atmosphere to the town. No matter how busy people are, they generally stop and listen for a few moments. Barrel organs have become so much a part of community life that even the burgomasters—the mayors of Dutch towns—often take part in the organ-grinders' competitions.

In the realm of music, the Dutch love of harmony has produced some of the best-loved orchestras in Europe, notably the Concertgebouw Orchestra of Amsterdam and the Residency Philharmonic Orchestra of The Hague. There are also a national opera, a Dutch ballet company, choral societies, and a horde of village bands. An organ festival is held at Haarlem every year.

There's music, too, in the chimes coming from churches, and there are carillon concerts in many town squares.

Thirteenth-century Holland survives in the Old Church at Delft, the final resting place of many national heroes.

HERO OF HAARLEM: NATIONAL IMAGE

FOR generations, the children of the world have become acquainted with their counterparts in Holland, like this bright-eyed lad, through the story of *Hans Brinker, or the Silver Skates*. Written almost a century ago by American author Mary Mapes Dodge, this classic tells the adventures of a boy growing up in the land of dikes and windmills and tulips.

Strangely enough, it is not Hans who remains in the memory, but a brief recounting within the book of the legend of the "Hero of Haarlem," the boy who saved his home town by putting his finger in a hole in the dike. As the tale goes, the boy, whose father was keeper of the canal locks of Haarlem, was on his way home at dusk one day. Noticing that the water was trickling through a tiny hole in the dike, he put his finger in the hole and held it there all night. At dawn, a passing minister saw the boy and relieved him. That's all there is to the story —yet it epitomizes the whole Dutch people in their courageous resistance to onslaught from the elements.

About ten years ago, in the village of Spaarndam (*spahrn*-DAHM) near Haarlem, a statue inspired by the story was erected. It is "Dedicated to Our Youth, to Honor the Boy Who Symbolizes the Eternal Struggle of Holland against the Sea." The boy at the dike may be a myth, but it's a myth with a profound meaning.

Haarlem, by the way, is one of the earliest centers of Dutch art, the city of Frans Hals and picturesque almshouses, the ancient residence of the Counts of Holland and one of the most attractive historic towns in the Netherlands. One of the outstanding sights is the Frans Hals Museum, which contains an unrivaled collection of paintings by that great master. You can view the paintings by candlelight while seventeenth-century music is played in the courtyard garden.

MARTYRED ARNHEM: OPEN-AIR MUSEUM

TODAY, the main attraction at Arnhem (ARN-*hem*) is the Open-Air Museum of Folklore and Customs, which overlooks the old town from a wooded hill. Here, assembled on a beautiful country estate, is everything about the national culture, character and peculiarities of Holland that you'd have to travel all across the nation to see: farm interiors where men and animals sleep under the same roof, trade and handicraft workshops, simple ovens and smithies, humble fishermen's huts, windmills, small bridges, magnificent dwellings of opulent merchants, costumes from various regions, relics of Holland's rural culture, even a complete transplanted street.

A somber glory weighs upon Arnhem. A historic battle started in September, 1944, when British paratroops—the Red Devils—supported by Polish units, landed in a clearing a few miles east of the town. The objective was to capture the bridge across the Rhine and hold it until Montgomery's Second Army arrived. When the Army's drive was delayed by the boggy terrain, the Red Devils were left without support and for nine days and nights they desperately resisted the German attacks, fighting in the streets, on the riverbanks and around the famous bridge. Although six thousand of its defenders lost their lives, the "Bridge of Martyrs" was blown up, and the great Arnhem square destroyed. Of Arnhem's twenty-eight thousand prewar houses, only one hundred forty-five were left undamaged.

Preserved at Arnhem is this old goose trap, an ingenious snare tunnel made of willows.

BYGONE PAGEANTRY: CASTLE AT DOORWERTH

WHILE we're at Arnhem, let's step over to the thirteenth-century castle of Doorwerth (DOHR-*vehrt*). Scene of heavy fighting during the airborne landings in the last war, the area around the castle took severe punishment. The cannons in the picture are part of the relics that remain. Today, the coach house of the castle houses a war museum.

Medieval castles like this one at Doorwerth are spotted throughout the Netherlands—grim as a prison, or gay and fairylike. Exuding memories of bygone glory and knightly magnificence, surrounded by protective moats and gardens the equal of Versailles, they seem to pop out of storybooks. Though without traditional ghosts as in English castles, they are full of historic treasures—antique furniture, golden goblets, elaborate chandeliers and mammoth fireplaces.

In several castles you can see the armor and weapons of the old Dutch knights. They re-create the days of chivalry and gallantry, of pomp and pageantry, forming the setting for jousting matches, tournaments, nobles contesting for palms of honor. From these castle gates, warriors departed on crusades to the Holy Land; feasts and ceremonies were celebrated in the great halls, attended by lackey, page and herald.

A few Dutch castles are still the homes of ancient noble families, but others are serving as schools or charitable institutions. Many, like Doorwerth, have been left in ruins by war and time.

Each preserved Dutch castle has its own history. Among the more exciting ones is the proud, imposing Muiderslot (*moy-dehr*-SLOHT), on the banks of the Vecht River just south of Amsterdam. With its wooden drawbridge, heavy gates, angular battlements and handsome turrets, Muiderslot is a splendid embodiment of the medieval dream castle.

ALKMAAR: AGE-OLD CHEESE MARKET

THIS is the celebrated cheese market in the lively old city of Alkmaar (AHLK-*mahr*) in the middle of North Holland province. Lying in the midst of rich pastures, Alkmaar is a leisurely three-hour trip from Amsterdam. Early on Fridays, from May to October, the market place is crowded with country folk. The cheese farmers come to town the night before in their odd market wagons, painted blue inside and loaded with the red or yellow globes of cheese. Others come via canals.

In this picture, the farmers are preparing to lay out their cheeses for sale. The luscious round cannon balls weigh slightly more than four pounds each, and those that are for export are painted a gleaming scarlet. Sales are completed with a handclasp. Later, the cheese porters, who are organized into a sort of medieval guild, toss them to the truck loaders as expertly as a troupe of jugglers. Then the cheeses roll on to the far corners of the earth.

The Friday morning market ritual ends with a delightful carillon concert at noon, with bells rung in the graceful weigh-house clock tower. The fine old carillon has mechanical puppets on horseback.

For Gouda cheese, familiar to everyone, the town of Gouda has its cheese market on Thursdays. There, the biggest cheeses weigh as much as forty-five pounds. The characteristic flavor of the Gouda cheeses is said to come from the special herbs and grasses on which the cows feed.

Costume and wares of the cheese vendors have gone unchanged for centuries.

53

THE HAGUE: PEACE PALACE

BUILT in pink and blue granite, the Peace Palace shown in this picture is the seat of the International Court of Justice and Permanent Court of Arbitration. It's in The Hague, where the Dutch government has its headquarters, including Parliament—although, curiously, the capital of the Netherlands is Amsterdam. The Hague's full name in Dutch is 's Gravenhage (SKRAH-*ven*-HAH-*keh*), meaning "The Count's Hedge," for it is believed that on this site there originally was a hunting lodge used by the Counts of Holland in the thirteenth century.

The stately Peace Palace has a spiritual tie to Americans: it was built in 1913 with $1,500,000 put up by Andrew Carnegie. Eleven nations contributed toward its decoration. From Germany came the wrought-iron door; Brazil gave rare woods; China, vases; Japan, embroideries; Italy, marble; France, tapestries; Spain, silverwork. Ironically, less than a year after the Palace was inaugurated with great ceremony as a symbol of peace, the First World War broke out.

Today, the Peace Palace contains the most comprehensive library on international law in the world, as well as many priceless gifts from various nations. It also houses the Academy of International Law, attended by some five hundred students.

As a city, The Hague itself has been called "the largest village in Europe" and it has the charm of a matron dressed in her Sunday best. It's the only place in western Holland which is not entirely built on piles—because it rests upon dune sand.

Also at The Hague you can see the Binnenhof (BIN-*nehn-hohff*), a remarkable group of buildings comprising the thirteenth-century "Hall of Knights." Nearby is the Mauritshuis (MOW-*rits-hoys*) Museum with its celebrated collection of Vermeer, Rembrandt and other old masters. The Hague is known for its fine avenues and its lovely parks and gardens.

54

LILLIPUTIAN TOWN: MADURODAM

HOLLAND in capsule form, a nation in a nutshell— that's the extraordinary Lilliputian town set up at Madurodam (*mah-doo-roh*-DAHM), on the outskirts of The Hague. It's the smallest "town" in the world, with everything built to a scale of one to twenty-five. It is not a copy of an actual town, but as a composite it is typical of the Netherlands.

Here are models of shops, farms, factories, houses dating from the Golden Century, a zoo, the Schiphol (SKIP-*hole*) airport near Amsterdam. Tiny ships move in and out of Rotterdam's realistic harbor. The Hague's Peace Palace tower clock shows the right time. An intricate railroad system, running over two and one-half miles of track, connects the minuscule villages and cities; trains pass under miniature bridges and whiz along the sides of canals with their moving barges. Organ music drifts out of a church where a wedding party is entering—and the church tower is no higher than your head. Grazing toy cows represent the nation's dairy industry. Windmills operate near fields of hyacinths and tulips.

At night, the town is illuminated with more than forty thousand lights. That's the best time to see it. Madurodam was built in 1952, and since then over 5,000,000 visitors, young and old, have gazed upon it in awe and delight.

Dreams come true for little girls in this city where all the houses are dollhouses.

SCHEVENINGEN: PLEASURE BY THE SEA

VIRTUALLY a part of The Hague, the seaside town of Scheveningen is a suburb with a split personality. Part of the community is a harbor district or fishing village—older than The Hague. There you can see the women still wearing their traditional costumes, generally in somber colors to show that their men have risked their lives on the unpredictable sea. The other part of Scheveningen is a worldly, fashionable resort. Facing the broad, sandy beaches is a long line of cosmopolitan hotels, smart restaurants and internationally renowned night clubs which attract holiday crowds from all parts of Holland and many other countries of Europe. Day or night, this sector of Scheveningen is always in high spirits.

Seeing gay Scheveningen today, you wouldn't guess that during the last war it was a bastion of Hitler's Atlantic Wall and was left a gaunt and desolate ruin. Its waterfront, then a mile of devastation, is now back to normal—except that some of the Victorian hotels have given way to modernity.

A special magnet for music lovers, who stream in from all over the world, is the annual "Holland Festival" from mid-June to mid-July. Many of the world's greatest musicians have performed at the festival, which is celebrated in both Amsterdam and Scheveningen, and the renowned Concertgebouw Orchestra gives several concerts in this seaside resort.

This part of Scheveningen contrasts sharply with the old part of town, where everything smells of fish and tar, and the wind-beaten men ignore the well-dressed (or scantily clad) visitors who crowd the beaches, boulevards and promenades.

MEI, 1940:
A CITY'S
AGONY

THIS statue in the center of Rotterdam is one of the most moving monuments in Europe. Called simply *Mei, 1940,* it commemorates that black Tuesday, May 14, 1940, when German bombers reduced the city to a wasteland of twisted steel and charred debris, destroying over 28,000 buildings—churches, hospitals, schools, shops and homes—in an area of 640 acres. The statue is a bronze female figure, her heart and half of her body torn out, looking up at the sky in agony and holding her palms aloft as if shielding her home against a rain of bombs.

As the end of World War II neared, the Germans proceeded to ravage the huge, throbbing harbor, too, blowing up the piers and other installations, blocking the Maas River with sunken ships. But with incredible, dynamic energy, Rotterdamers—aided by Marshall Plan funds —rebuilt the vast port.

Today, all around the tortured face and body of *Mei, 1940,* people go about their business in a fresh setting of steel and glass, brick and concrete. Some of the finest shops in the city are clustered in shopping pavilions, in which automobiles are prohibited so as to permit carefree window-shopping.

Appropriately, when Queen Wilhelmina came back to her country after five years of wartime exile, she bestowed on Rotterdam the right to use as its motto, *"Sterker Door Strijd"* (STEHR-*kehr* DOOR STRAID)— "Stronger Through Struggle."

Reconstructed Rotterdam is an ultramodern city, where only memories of prewar days remain.

ROTTERDAM: A PHOENIX FROM THE ASHES

THIS is a glimpse of the harbor of Rotterdam today, the sight of children playing on the docks a symbol of the peace and prosperity that has come to the reborn city. Newly widened and deepened waterways carry the seaborne traffic, and once again the harbor is heavy with shipping, since Rotterdam is the second largest seaport in the world. An average of sixty-three seagoing ships enter the harbor each day, plus about five hundred barges and other inland traffic from the Rhine River.

Construction never stops in Rotterdam. New industries are going up along the eighteen miles from the town to its sea outlet. A new "Europoort" (oy-*roh-pohrt*), where the waterway from Rotterdam meets the sea, is taking shape as a Gateway-to-Europe harbor for the six-nation Common Market.

In the city, the old town exists only as a nostalgic memory. Dutch architects went all out to design a contemporary architecture to demonstrate the progressive and aesthetic culture of the new Netherlands. Café-restaurants, banks and office buildings reflect the ultramodern trend.

Before the war, crowded slums—some dating back to the Middle Ages—sheltered many of the one hundred thousand Rotterdamers who lived in the central city. Today, modern apartments have been provided for twenty thousand, while the rest live in a ring of low-rent garden suburbs and homes that offer space, air and playgrounds for the young, apartments without stairs for the old.

Rotterdam, a symphony in concrete, glass and stone, is now wholly new. The rebuilding of this stricken city is a miracle of enterprise.

ENKHUIZEN: FISHING VILLAGE

LET'S move on to the dreamy fishing village of Enkhuizen on the Zuider Zee. During the Golden Age of the seventeenth century, spice-laden ships from the Dutch East Indies put into this port. Today, the richest and most characteristic Zuider Zee community is Enkhuizen, one of the few places on the coast which will retain access to the open sea after the ambitious Dutch plans for land reclamation have been completed.

At Enkhuizen there are still fishermen, although in the other towns on the coast the industry is said to be doomed. Come spring, while the women are mending their nets, the men begin to feel "herring sick"— a malady which is nothing more than intense longing for the sea. Furiously they start cleaning and shining up their boats. Then, on the Saturday designated as "Flag Day," the freshly painted and gaily decorated vessels are ready to sail out, an event which draws throngs each year. On Sunday, churches offer special services for the safe return of all. In the afternoon, everyone goes walking around the harbor—the fishermen with their wives and children, the younger men with girls on their arms. Next day, the fleets put out to sea, waved "Godspeed!" by their folk.

Rugged individualists, the fisherfolk of Enkhuizen earn a scanty living, but they're happier than they would be with higher wages working in a shipping company. They are a race of optimists and console themselves over failures with the saying, "Fish have fins," meaning they have swum away, and resign themselves good-humoredly to their disappointment. "In the morning," they'll say, "you will find where you should have been at night."

Curiously, most of the fishermen haven't learned to swim—they feel so perfectly at home on the sea that the thought of danger rarely occurs to them.

NATIONAL DELICACY: HERRING BY THE BARREL

"A HERRING a day keeps the doctor away," say the Dutch. These barrels of herring being sealed are destined for the gullets of Netherlanders who like to eat them for lunch, as a snack between meals, or as a nutritious dinner course.

One off-beat sight common on Dutch streets is the spectacle of a passer-by stopping at a vendor's stall to buy a few herring and eat them on the spot. The fishmonger scales and guts the cured, uncooked fish, dividing them in halves with an intricate flick. Then the buyer delicately holds up a tender, tangy fish by the tail, dips it in a plate of raw onions and swallows it in two mouthfuls. Everyone does it in Holland, including business executives and the Queen's ministers.

Fishing for herring is done in the North Sea, and in a good year about a billion herring are caught, roughly half going for export. The first arrival of the glistening catch in May is greeted by the fishmongers with carts flying the national colors. By tradition, the first barrel of fish is formally offered to the Queen.

As far as flavor and quality are concerned, the Dutch herring can compete with its more elegant brother, the salmon. A whole process of curing precedes the sale of the so-called "raw" herring on city streets. This gives the Dutch herring that very special fresh and delicate flavor. At least one Dutch town carries three crossed herring in its coat of arms.

ROYAL PARADE: THE QUEEN'S BIRTHDAY

EVERY year on April 30th, the birthday of Queen Juliana, a parade is held before the Palace of Soestdijk (*soost*-DAIK). For the occasion, many Hollanders bring armfuls of flowers to streets that become a sea of flags and pennants. Soestdijk is Holland's royal village where Queen Juliana, Prince Bernhard and their daughters live modestly in the charming royal residence. The Queen and her consort have lived there since their marriage, except for the wartime years when they were in Canada. If you should see a healthy girl walking through the village, carrying some schoolbooks under her arm, it may well be one of the princesses.

Although the Queen and her family live at Soestdijk, they have a town castle in Amsterdam, which is the "official" residence but serves mainly constitutional needs. At The Hague, when the Royal Family comes on a visit, thousands of people come out to press against barriers, waiting until the open carriages of the royal pair and the princesses appear. Once a year, on the third Tuesday of September, the Queen opens the national parliament at The Hague in a brilliant ceremony.

The Netherlands is a constitutional monarchy, with the executive power in the hands of a Cabinet based on a parliamentary majority. The legislature consists of two houses—the First Chamber and the Second Chamber, both elected by popular vote in a system of proportional representation. The Queen signs all bills approved by the legislature. Beyond all partisan strife, she stands for unity of the country.

FLOWERLAND FANTASY: KEUKENHOF GARDENS

"A TONIC, an inspiration and a message of beauty"—that's what the Keukenhof (KUH-*ken-hohff*) Gardens have been called. Here at Lisse (LISS-*eh*), halfway between Haarlem and Leiden (LIE-*den*), is the remarkable sixty-two-acre baronial flower park. In a blaze of color, miles of winding paths are lined with beds, borders and seemingly casual patches of millions of crocuses, narcissuses, hyacinths, tulips and many lesser known spring flowers.

The most valuable blooms are housed in giant greenhouses frequently containing more than thirty-five thousand tulips of seven hundred varieties, each with a unique breeding history. A pavilion demonstrates what can be done in the art of floral decoration. In spring, when the rippling botanical fantasy is open to the public, it is transformed into perfumed loveliness.

Keukenhof, which means "kitchen garden," was once part of the hunting domain of a Bavarian countess who had a castle nearby. Her kitchens were supplied with game from the Keukenhof woods.

Besides the Keukenhof Gardens, flower lovers will get a thrill out of the daily flower auctions at Aalsmeer (AHLS-*mehr*), some ten miles southwest of Amsterdam. The amazing profusion of floral beauty to be seen at these auctions, where mountains of blooms are sold every morning, is unforgettable. Aalsmeer is the most gigantic flower shop on the continent, and it has the largest glasshouse garden in all Europe.

Infinite varieties of tulips have been developed through the years by patient Dutch flower breeders.

A HOME IN LISSE: A PLEASURE TO THE EYE

HERE we see a fairly typical bulb grower's home in Lisse, heart of the bulb fields. From the lowly to the richest, the Dutchman spares nothing to make his home clean, comfortable and friendly because the people are essentially family folk. Inside, the atmosphere is cozy: the immaculate kitchen has scrubbed flagstones, chinaware glistens on the shelves. Houses of upper-bracket families are of brick, stone or cement, with attractive tiled roofs, though often they have no central heating; instead they have a Dutch-type oil-coal stove in each room except the bedrooms. In the suburbs of big cities, the houses are surrounded by well-kept gardens.

The Dutch reputation for cleanliness is reflected in the word *schoon* (SKOHN), which means both clean and beautiful. With constant dusting, scrubbing and polishing, the Dutch housewife makes her home a pleasure to the eye. Saturday is a nation-wide *Schoonmaakdag* (SKOHN-*mahk-dahk*)—"clean-making day"—when even the pavement in front of the house gets a good scouring. This finicky neatness is a form of thrift, for it preserves precious possessions. In some homes, blinds are lowered so that the furniture upholstery doesn't fade. The well-educated Hollanders today, however, prefer the discoloring light to the thrifty darkness.

The owner of the house in this picture, one of 25,000 full-time bulb workers, is descended from generations of bulb growers. While much of the skill has been handed down from father to son, many young men receive professional training at government horticultural schools and Dutch scientists are constantly improving the quality of the bulbs. Workers like these, and their bulb fields nearby, have made the name of Holland renowned throughout the world.

73

LOVE OF
BEAUTY:
THE DUTCH
SOUL

HERE in this vividly colorful picture you can detect the innate love of the Dutch people for beauty. The young man on the barge is carrying off the flower harvest, poling his way through the intricate network of canals that crisscross the bulb fields. Each spring, as soon as the tulips, hyacinths and other bulb flowers reach full bloom, the flowers are cut off. This is done to permit all the strength to go into the bulbs that eventually will be exported to the world.

With these blooms, schoolchildren, merchants and home owners will then create magical mosaics in a wide variety of natural and geometric designs—always a breath-taking sight for visitors as well as for Hollanders themselves. Other flowers will be formed into garlands and leis. If you come to Holland in the spring, you'll probably be garlanded with a lei as you step off your plane, as if you were in Hawaii.

The flowers in the field behind the barge are among several thousand varieties of tulips and other bulb flowers created by Dutch bulb scientists. The sandy soil in this section is ideal for growing these blossoms, so glorious that you almost wonder if they're real.

There are tense moments in the flower auctions at Aalsmeer, where blossoms are big business.

All over the world, Dutch bulbs planted in the fall bloom in the spring to salute the undying spirit of Hollanders. This picture epitomizes the spirit of the nation: emerging from the long struggles of the past, the Dutch today enjoy the living beauty of their radiant country.

74

BULB LAND: FABULOUS FLOWER FESTIVAL

HOLLAND is a country of flowers the year round and they are a part of every Dutchman's life. In spring especially, when the bulb fields are in bloom, the country—spreading out its colorful carpet—is fabulously beautiful. Thousands of acres are transformed into a sea of delicate yellow, salmon-pink, brilliant red, blue-black and pure white blossoms.

Toward the end of April, busloads of visitors come from all over Europe to view the unforgettable spectacle. The Flower Festival Pageant usually takes place on the last Saturday in April, with scores of flower-bedecked floats designed around a central theme, such as "Holland is the Bride," or "Flower Paradise." In this picture, you see one of these magnificent creations.

Floral floats are a Dutch specialty at festivals in towns around the bulb fields—Lisse, Sassenheim (SASS-*sen-haim*) and Hillegom (HILL-*leh-kohm*)—where tens of thousands of people will line the route. Houses, too, are decorated with floral festoons and bouquets, displaying ingenious lawn mosaics entirely made of blossoms. How can the Dutch afford to "waste" millions of blooms just for beauty's sake? Actually, they are not spending blooms, for these are the flowers removed from bulbs planned for export. Instead of throwing them away, the shrewd Dutch utilize the flowers for the Festivals to promote the bulb industry. And it's a big industry, too, creating three billion bulbs each year; the Associated Bulb Growers of Holland export some $60,000,000 in bulbs.

The gay atmosphere of the Flower Festivals captures everyone who watches, and it's bound to make you feel the heartbeat of this neat and joyful little country.

THE GENTLE
PEOPLE:
HEALTHY
YOUTH

GOLDEN-HAIRED and rosy-cheeked, the youngsters of Holland depict the radiant health and hardihood of the people. Until they are five or six, children in some villages dress almost alike in skirts and wear long hair. Boys are distinguished by a small star or round patch on their hat and by a stripe on their shirt or blouse. In some outlying communities, there's no drastic change of attire until the youngsters reach the age of eighteen.

With its high birth rate, Holland has more young people than any other country in Western Europe. Mothers spend a great deal of time with their children, who are always uncommonly courteous, usually shy with strangers, friendly but with a quiet reserve. Even in the radiance of their youth, the Dutch maintain their dignity.

The children of Holland learn very early the rich heritage of their land and the solid virtues of the Dutch—a free spirit combined with hardheaded practicality and strong ties to home and country. Patient, hard-working and cheerful, they remember to thank God and also to help themselves. Clearly the difficult position of this small nation, uncomfortably close to more powerful states and ever threatened by the hungry sea, has developed in her people an appreciation for life and a drive toward survival that may explain the invincibility of the Dutch.

Perhaps the singular durability of this people was best expressed by the poet Potgieter, in these lines written in 1832:

> Gray is thy sky and stormy thy strand,
> Bare are thy dunes and flat thy meadows,
> Nature hath made thee with a grudging hand,
> Yet I intensely love thee, my land.
> All that thou art is our forefathers' work....

78

SOME FAMOUS NAMES IN DUTCH HISTORY

DESIDERIUS ERASMUS (1466?-1536)—*Great humanist, philosopher and scholar, whose literary talent and devotion to freedom made him one of the eminent men of his age.*

WILLIAM THE SILENT (1533-1584)—*Prince of Orange, founder of the Dutch Republic and first stadholder (chief executive officer). "Father of his Country." Opposed Philip II's persecution of Protestants in Orange and Holland, led the War of Liberation against the Duke of Alva and Spanish armies.*

JAN VAN OLDEN BARNEVELDT (1547-1619)—*Statesman, champion of Dutch independence. Opposed policies of Maurice of Nassau, negotiated treaty with Spain.*

JACOBUS ARMINIUS (1560-1609)—*Theologian, professor at Leiden University, leader of Remonstrants, a religious sect which favored theory of universal redemption.*

MAURICE OF NASSAU (1567-1625)—*Stadholder of Dutch Republic. Great military leader, defeating Spain at Turnhout (1597) and at Nieuport (1600). Agreed to truce after losing Ostend (1604) but later renewed struggle.*

FRANS HALS (1580?-1666)—*Among the greatest Dutch painters of portraits and everyday scenes.*

HUGO GROTIUS (1583-1645)—*One of the founders of the science of international law. Condemned to life imprisonment as leader of the Remonstrants but escaped to France where he wrote* De Jure Belli et Pacis.

FREDERICK HENRY (1584-1647)—*Prince of Orange, brother of Maurice, stadholder for quarter-century when Golden Age of Republic set in.*

REMBRANDT VAN RIJN (1606-1669)—*Painter and etcher. Leading representative of the Dutch school of painting, and master of light and shadow.*

JAN DE WITT (1625-1672)—*Prime Minister of Holland, who concluded peace with England and strengthened commercial supremacy in East.*

WILLIAM II OF ORANGE (1626-1650)—*Stadholder who attempted to make himself sovereign; after his death, stadholdership was temporarily suspended.*

CHRISTIAN HUYGENS (1629-1695)—*Physicist, astronomer, mathematician. First to use pendulum to regulate movement of clocks.*

BARUCH SPINOZA (1632-1677)—*Philosopher, regarded as the most eminent exponent of pantheism.*

JAN VERMEER (1632-1675)—*Painter of life-sized figures, interiors and landscapes.*

ANTON VAN LEEUWENHOEK (1632-1723)—*Pioneer scientist; made simple microscope and observed microorganisms with it; first to describe red blood corpuscles.*

JAN SWAMMERDAM (1637-1680)—*Naturalist, known for biological researches with microscope and study of the anatomy of insects.*

WILLIAM III OF ORANGE (1650-1702)—*Stadholder of Holland and King of England (1689-1702).*

VINCENT VAN GOGH (1853-1890)—*Painter, etcher, lithographer. Associated with postimpressionist school.*

HENDRIK ANTOON LORENTZ (1853-1928)—*Physicist who helped develop the electron theory of matter. Shared 1902 Nobel Prize in physics.*

WILHELMINA (1880-   )—*First Queen of Netherlands (1890-1948). Reigned throughout first four decades of this century.*

JULIANA (1909-   )—*Present Queen of the Netherlands. Only daughter of Wilhelmina, ascended the throne in 1948.*

SOME FAMOUS DATES IN DUTCH HISTORY

57 B.C.	*Julius Caesar invades the region of the Netherlands, which becomes part of the Roman world.*
843 A.D.	*The Frankish empire, which had controlled the area since the downfall of Rome, breaks up. The Netherlands is split between Eastern and Western Franks, or Germany and France.*
c. 900	*Swept by Danish invaders, the Netherlands becomes a land of many independent feudal states. Starting in the twelfth century, towns rise to an important position, with a new middle class of tradesmen.*
1566	*Spain takes possession of the Netherlands, and curbs religious and political freedom.*
1579	*History of new republic starts with Union of Utrecht, confederating the rebellious northern provinces.*
1581	*Northern provinces sever all ties with Spain and declare themselves the Republic of the United Netherlands.*
1596	*Triple Alliance with France and England against Spain marks recognition of the Netherlands as a sovereign power.*
1595-8	*First Dutch voyage to East Indies. United Dutch East India Company founded, 1602.*
1600's	*Golden Age, when Rembrandt, Hals and Vermeer produce their masterpieces. Dutch fleet commands the seas and establishes colonies throughout the world, from New Amsterdam to New Zealand.*
1795	*After a century of decline, caused by dissension within and attack from without, the Dutch Republic is conquered by France.*
1815	*The Netherlands becomes an independent constitutional monarchy. William VI of Orange crowned as head of state, uniting all the Netherlands.*
1830	*Southern part of the Netherlands revolts to become the kingdom of Belgium.*
1920	*The Netherlands joins the League of Nations, discarding its policy of passive neutrality maintained through World War I.*
1940	*Holland is invaded by Germany.*
1945	*Allied offensive against Third Reich liberates occupied Holland.*
1948	*The Netherlands joins with Belgium and Luxembourg in an economic union called Benelux. Queen Wilhelmina abdicates in favor of her daughter Juliana.*
1949	*The Netherlands Indies becomes completely independent republic, called Indonesia.*
1954	*Holland grants greater independence to Dutch Guiana and the Netherlands Antilles.*

SOME DUTCH WORDS AND PHRASES

Here is a list of words and phases that would be handy when visiting the Netherlands. The words are given in English and Dutch and then in simple phonetics, with the accented syllable in small capitals.

Do you speak Dutch?	Spreekt U Nederlands?	*(sprehkt ew* NEH-*dehr-lants)*
How do you say . . . .?	Hoe zegt U. . . .?	*(hoo sehkht ew)*
What do you wish?	Wat wenst U?	*(vaht vehnst ew)*
Where is. . . .?	Waar is. . . .?	*(vahr is)*
How far?	Hoe ver?	*(hoo fair)*
Near (to)	Dicht by. . . .	*(deekht bay)*
Far (from)	Ver van. . . .	*(fehr fahn)*

English	Dutch	Pronunciation
How long? (time)	Hoe lang?	*(hoo lahng)*
I want. . . .	Ik wens. . . .	*(ick vehns)*
I have. . . .	Ik heb. . . .	*(ick hep)*
Excuse me.	Neemt U my niet kwalyk.	*(nehmt ew may neet K'VAH-lewk)*
I do not understand.	Ik kan het niet verstaan.	*(eek kahn heht neet fehr-STAHN)*
Can you help me?	Kunt U my helpen?	*(kewnt ew may HEHL-pen)*
How much is it?	Wat kost dat?	*(vaht kohst daht)*
Thanks (very much).	Dank U (zeer).	*(dahn-KEW) (zehr)*
Yes. No.	Ja. Nee.	*(YAH) (NAY)*
Perhaps.	Misschien.	*(miss-s'KHEEN)*
Enough. Too much.	Genoeg. Te veel.	*(kheh-NOOKH) (tuh feel)*
Now. Later.	Nu. Later.	*(NEW) (LAH-tehr)*
Good. Better.	Goed. Beter.	*(KHOOD) (BEH-tehr)*
Bad. Worse.	Slecht. Slechter.	*(SLEHKHT) (SLEHKH-tehr)*
Hello (good day).	Dag! (goede dag)	*(DAH-ahkh) (KHOO-yeh dahkh)*
Train Airplane	Trein Vliegtuig	*(TRAYN) (FLEEKH-toykh)*
Bus Boat	Bus Boot	*(BEWS) (BOAT)*
Ticket Ticket office	Kaartje Loket	*(KAHRT-yeh) (loh-KETT)*
Hotel Room	Hotel Kamer	*(hoh-TEL) (KAH-mehr)*
Breakfast	Ontbijt	*(ohnt-BAIT)*
Baggage Customs	Bagage Douane	*(bah-KHAH-zheh) (doo-AH-neh)*
The washroom	Toilet	*(twah-LET)*
Ladies'. . . . Men's. . . .	Dames. . . . Heren. . . .	*(DAH-mess) (HEH-rehn)*

NUMBERS

English	Dutch	Pronunciation
One	Een	*(EHN)*
Two	Twee	*(TVEH)*
Three	Drie	*(DREE)*
Four	Vier	*(FEAR)*
Five	Vijf	*(FAIF)*
Six	Zes	*(ZEHS)*
Seven	Zeven	*(ZEE-vehn)*
Eight	Acht	*(AHKHT)*
Nine	Negen	*(NEE-khehn)*
Ten	Tien	*(TEEN)*
Hundred	Honderd	*(HOHN-dehrt)*
Thousand	Duizend	*(DOY-zehnt)*

DAYS OF THE WEEK

English	Dutch	Pronunciation
Sunday	Zondag	*(ZOHN-dahkh)*
Monday	Maandag	*(MAHN-dahkh)*
Tuesday	Dinsdag	*(DINS-dahkh)*
Wednesday	Woensdag	*(VOONS-dahkh)*
Thursday	Donderdag	*(DOHN-dehr-dahkh)*
Friday	Vrijdag	*(FRAY-dahkh)*
Saturday	Zaterdag	*(ZAH-tehr-dahkh)*

MONEY

Gulden	*(KHEWL-dehn)*	100 Dutch cents
Stuiver	*(STOY-vehr)*	Dutch 5-cent piece
Dubbeltje	*(DEWB-belt-yeh)*	Dutch 10 cents
Kwartje	*(KVAHRT-yeh)*	Dutch 25 cents

INDEX

83